紫禁城

THE FORBIDDEN CITY

故宫博物院
紫禁城出版社

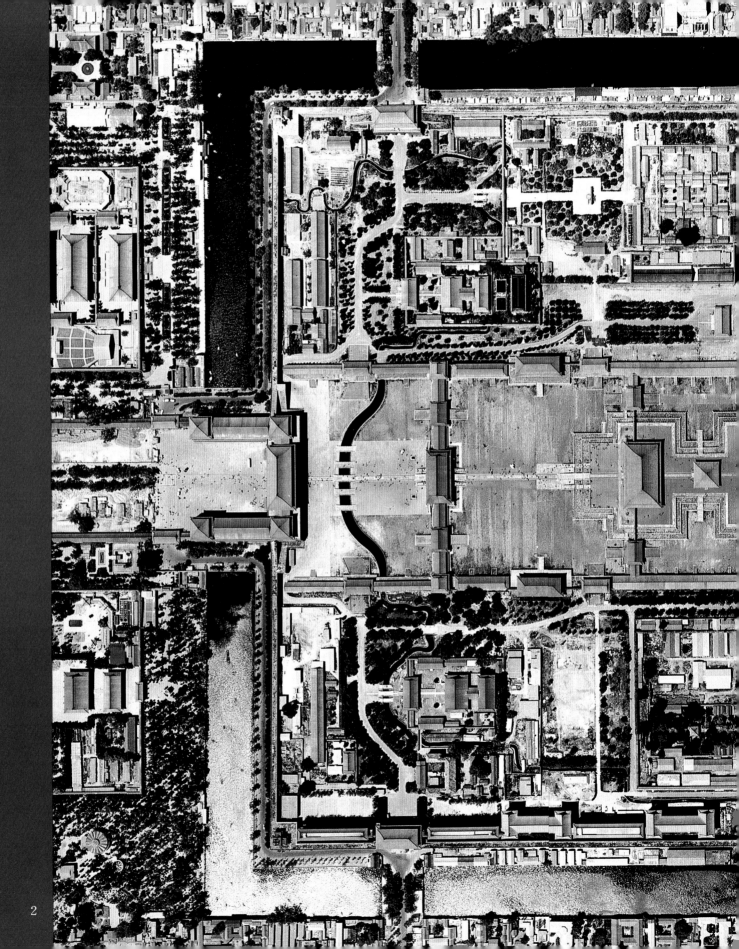

3 紫禁城鳥瞰

紫禁城平面爲長方形，佔地七十二萬多平方米，共有四門：正南的午門是紫禁城的正門，東爲東華門，西爲西華門，北爲玄武門（清康熙年間，因避玄燁之諱，改名神武門）。其中的午門，並不是我國舊小說、戲劇中常說的"推出午門斬首"的地方，祇是明代對官員施行特有的刑罰即"廷杖"的場所。

紫禁城鳥瞰

紫禁城の平面は長方形で、敷地面積は七十二万平方メートルを越え、四面にはそれぞれ一つ、計四つの門がある。そのうちの正南の午門が紫禁城の正門であり、東は東華門、西は西華門、北は玄武門（清の康熙年間に、玄燁という皇帝の名をはばかって、神武門と改めた）である。中国の昔の小説や芝居をみると、「午門を推し出して、首を斬る」という言葉がよくでてくる。しかし、紫禁城の午門は、明代には罪を犯した役人に「廷杖」という特有の罰を加える場所であったこともあるが、別に首を斬る場所であったわけではない。

Bird's-eye view of the Forbidden City.

Occupying a rectangular area of more than 720,000 square metres, the Forbidden City has four entrance gates: the main Meridian Gate (Wumen) to the south, the Eastern Flower Gate (Donghuamen), the Western Flower Gate (Xihuamen), and the Gate of Divine Prowess (Shenwumen) to the north.

展現在你面前的這本畫册，介紹的是明清兩代的皇宮紫禁城，即故宮，現在是故宮博物院所在地。

紫禁城宮殿是明代第三個皇帝朱棣下令營建的，於永樂十八年（1420年）底基本建成。第二年，明代京都正式從南京遷到北京。

紫禁城位於北京城的中心，建築規模之巨，擧世無雙。明清兩代，先後有二十四個皇帝住在這裏。深宮禁掖，闈幕又厚又嚴，內景如何？看了這本畫册，或許會解開你心頭之謎。

ここに紹介するのは、明・清両王朝の皇宮——紫禁城である。昔の皇居を意味する故宮の名で呼ばれ、今は故宮博物院になっている。

紫禁城宮殿の造営を命じたのは、明の第三代皇帝朱棣、つまり永楽皇帝で、永楽十八年（1420年）末にほぼ完成した。翌十九年（1421年）、明の都は正式に南京から北京に移った。

北京城の中央にある紫禁城は、建築規模の大きさからいって、世界にならぶものがない。ここには、明・清両王朝のあわせて二十四代の皇帝がかつて住んでいたが、それだけに、宮殿は奥深く、十重二十重の壁をめぐらした中をうかがい知ることはできなかった。一体どうなっているのだろうか。この問いに答えるのが本書である。

The Imperial Palace, home of the emperors of the Ming and Qing dynasties and known also as the Forbidden City, now houses the Palace Museum.

Construction of the Imperial Palace was started by order of the third Ming emperor, Yongle, and was basically completed near the end of 1420, the eighteenth year of Emperor Yongle's reign. The following year the Ming Dynasty officially moved its capital from Nanjing to Beijing.

Biggest complex of its kind in the world, the Forbidden City was situated in the centre of Beijing. Twenty-four Ming and Qing emperors resided there. What was it like behind the carefully guarded tall, thick walls of the Forbidden City? This volume will give you a clue to the mystery.

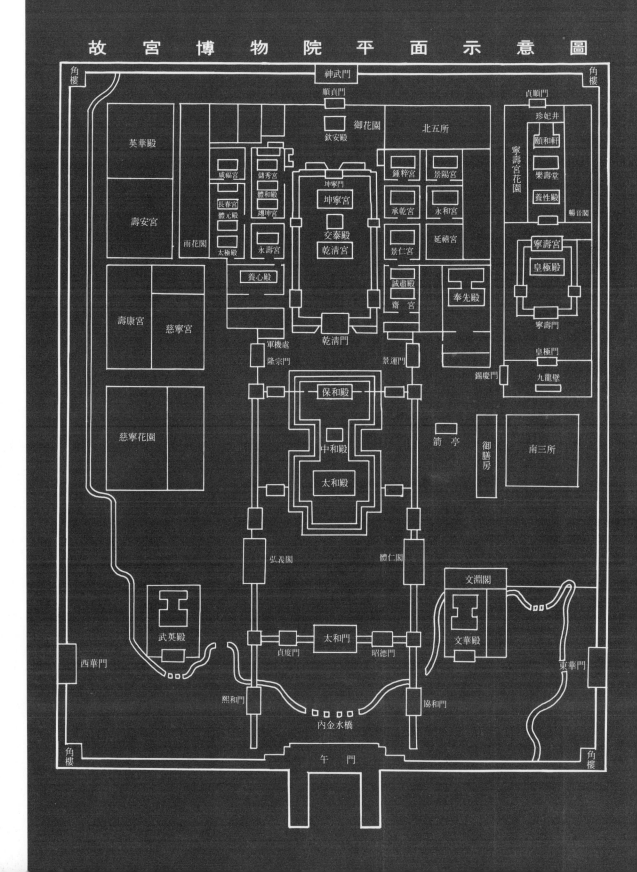

故 宮 博 物 院 平 面 示 意 圖

外

城

5 紫禁城正門——午門遠眺
紫禁城の正門—午門の遠景
Distant view of Meridian Gate — the main entrance
to the Forbidden City.

6 午門一角
午門（部分）
Part of Meridian Gate.

7　　有三層重簷、七十二條脊，結構精巧、造
型優美的角樓

三重の屋根、計72本の棟からできた、構造、
造形ともにきわめて精巧な角楼

With three-tiered eaves and seventy-two ridges, the northeast corner tower stands out for its ingenious structure and beautiful shape.

8 從景山遠眺神武門
景山から神武門をのぞむ
A distant view of the Gate of Divine Prowess from Coal Hill (Jingshan).

臘月的紫禁城
十二月の紫禁城
The Forbidden City in the dead of winter.

前三殿

走進午門，登上太和門，放眼北望，眺過
開闊肅穆的廣場，就能看到在三重漢白玉石雕
欄環繞的"工"字形高大臺基上，矗立着一座
莊嚴宏偉的宮殿，這就是太和殿。

　午門をくぐり、太和門に立てば、北側にひ
ろびろとした広場がひろがり、さらにその先
に宏壮な宮殿があたりを威圧して立っている
のが見える。漢白玉の石刻欄干をめぐらせた
上下三層の「工」字形の大きな石造基壇の上
に立つこの宮殿が世に知られる太和殿であ
る。

　After going through Meridian Gate, one comes to
the Gate of Supreme Harmony (Taihemen). Standing
at the top of the gate and looking northward across
a vast courtyard, one finds a magnificent building set
prominently on broad I-shaped terraces composed
of three layers of white marble, each layer surrounded by a balustrade. This is the Hall of Supreme
Harmony.

12

13

12 太和門廣場雪景
太和門広場の雪景色
Snowy courtyard of the Gate of Supreme Harmony.

13 内金水橋景觀
内金水橋
Bridges over the Inner Golden River.

14 從太和門回首看午門
太和門から見た午門
View of Meridian Gate from the Gate of Supreme
Harmony.

15 蜿蜒的内金水河
えんえんと流れる内金水河
The meandering Inner Golden River.

16 太和門前銅獅
太和門前の銅獅子
Bronze lion in front of the Gate
of Supreme Harmony.

19 三臺上的漢白玉石欄杆
　三層の基壇にめぐらされた漢白玉欄干
White marble balustrades.

清代には、重要な儀式ともなれば、文武百官が太和殿前の広場に集まり、官位別を示す銅製の標識──品級山にしたがって、正・従一品から九品まであわせて十八階級にわかれて、順序よく立ちならんだものであった。

For grand ceremonies during the Qing Dynasty civil and military officials lined up according to rank in the vast courtyard in front of the Hall of Supreme Harmony. Their positions were designated by bronze markers, ranging from the first to the ninth rank.

20 蔚爲壯觀的太和殿
壯大な太和殿
The magnificent Hall of Supreme Harmony (Taihe-dian), popularly known as the Hall of the Golden Throne (Jinluandian).

清代舉行大典時，文武百官要在太和殿前廣場上集合，按銅鑄品級山上標誌的正、從一至九品共十八班，依次站好。

紫禁城的建築布局分外朝和內廷兩大部份。外朝在南面，又稱前朝，主體建築有三大殿，皇帝登極、祝壽、大婚等重大典禮在這裏進行。內廷在乾清門廣場以北，包括後三宮、養心殿、東西六宮以及後三宮東西兩側的寧壽宮、慈寧宮等，是皇帝和后妃們居住的地方。

21 太和殿內景
太和殿の内部
Interior view of the Hall of Supreme Harmony.

紫禁城の建物は、外朝と内廷の二大部分からなる。外朝は南の方にあって、前朝とも呼ばれる。三大殿がその中心的建築で、皇帝の即位式、誕生日祝い、婚礼など重要な式典がここでおこなわれた。乾清門広場から北は内廷で、ここには後三宮、養心殿、東・西六宮および後三宮の東西両側に並ぶ寧寿宮、慈寧宮などがある。皇帝や皇后・妃嬪たちが日常起居していた場所である。

The palace grounds are divided into two parts: the Front Palace (Qianchao) to the south and the Inner Palace (Neiting) to the north. The Front Palace consists chiefly of the three great halls — the Hall of Supreme Harmony (Taihedian), the Hall of Central Harmony (Zhonghedian), and the Hall of Preserving Harmony (Baohedian). Here important ceremonies, such as the accession of a new emperor to the throne and the emperor's birthday and wedding, were held.

From the Gate of Heavenly Purity (Qianqingmen) northward is the Inner Palace, including the Palace of Heavenly Purity (Qiangqingong), the Hall of Prosperity (Jiaotaidian), the Hall of Earthly Tranquility (Kunninggong), the Hall of Mental Cultivation (Yangxindian), the six eastern halls and the six western halls, the Palace of Tranquility and Longevity (Ningshougong), and the Palace of Benevolent Peace (Cininggong). The Inner Palace was the residential area of the emperor and imperial household.

22 從寶座背後看太和殿藻井

玉座の背後から見た太和殿の藻井（装飾天井）

View of the coffered ceiling in the Hall of Supreme Harmony from behind the throne.

23 金漆蟠龍寶座與金漆雕龍圍屏

透かし彫りに金漆をほどこした蟠竜模様の玉座と竜を彫刻した金漆の背屏風

The golden lacquerware throne with coiling dragons, backed by a golden lacquerware screen carved with dragons.

太和殿是三大殿的主殿，其規模、造型、裝飾和陳設，無不着意安排，採用了顯示皇權至高無上的最高規格。

皇帝在太和殿舉行朝賀大典的情景又怎樣呢？明代，要事先把寶座、御案、香案、樂器、鹵簿（即儀仗）等都準備齊全，屆時捶三鼓、奏中和韶樂、三鳴鞭，然後進表、宣表、致詞……跪拜、三呼萬歲，最後皇帝降座回華蓋殿（清初改名中和殿）。清代舉行大典的儀式承襲明制，祇是略有變更。

太和殿內氣派非凡，金光燦燦。正中高臺上安放金漆蟠龍寶座及金漆雕龍圍屏，兩旁有六根瀝粉貼金蟠龍金柱。正對寶座上方，有一顆銀白色的大圓珠，從藻井的金漆蟠龍口裏垂下。

大臣們難得見上皇帝一面。大典時文武官員祇能站在丹陛之下的廣場上，如果被召到殿內寶座前，那就是極大的榮耀與恩典。

寶座前兩側安放着四種成對的陳設品，寶座高臺下階前陳設鼎式香爐。這些陳設品有神鳥異獸、仿古彝器，寓意吉祥長壽。

太和殿前的丹墀（俗稱月臺）上，陳設日晷、嘉量、銅鼎、銅龜、銅鶴，象徵江山萬代永固，皇帝萬壽無疆。每逢大典，爐、龜、鶴內都要點燃香料，煙霧繚繞，增添肅穆神秘氣氛。

太和殿之後是中和殿、保和殿。

太和殿は三大殿のなかの主殿であって、規模、造型、裝飾、設備といずれをとりあげてみても、十分に念を入れてねりあげたものであって、絶大な皇帝の権威を示す最高の格式をもちいている。

太和殿で朝賀の大典をおこなうときは、いったいどのような様子だったのであろうか。明代には、まず玉座、机、香机、楽器、儀仗などすべて用意をととのえておく。時間になると、大鼓を三度たたき、中和韶楽を奏し、鞭を三度ならす。それから、上奏がおこなわれ、宣旨があり、ことばのやりとりをし、……そして、ひざまずいて皇帝を拝礼し、万歳を三唱し、最後に皇帝が玉座をおりて、華蓋殿（清の初期に中和殿と改称）にもどるという順序であった。清代になってからも、大典の儀式は明代のそれと同じだったが、細かいところにはある程度の変更もあった。

太和殿の内部は金色にかがやき、豪華な感じにあふれている。正面の高い台座の上には金の漆をほどこした蟠竜模様の玉座と竜の彫刻をほどこした金の漆の背屏風がおかれ、その両側には、やはり竜をめぐらせた金箔漆塗りの柱が立っている。玉座の真上では、藻井（装飾天井）の金漆蟠竜が口で銀白色の大きな珠をつりおろしている。

大臣でも、やたらに皇帝に会えるわけではない。文官、武官たちは、大典の時にも宮殿の表の台の下の広場に並ばせてもらえるだけであって、とくに皇帝のお声がかりで、太和殿のなかの玉座の前まで入ることを許されたなら、それこそ最大の栄誉であり、恩典であった。

玉座の前方両側には四対の置物が、また玉座台座の前には鼎の形をした香炉が置いてある。神鳥、異獣、あるいは大昔の彝器をかたどったこうした置物は、吉祥、長寿をあらわすものである。

太和殿前の広い台——丹墀（俗に月台ともいう）には、日晷、嘉量、銅鼎、銅亀、銅鶴などが並べられてある。これは御代が永くつづき、皇帝がいつまでも長寿するようという意味をあらわしている。大典ともなれば、これら銅炉、銅亀、銅鶴で香がたかれ、そこから漂い出る紫煙が荘厳さにいっそう色を添える。

太和殿の後ろに見えるのが、中和殿と保和殿である。

24 盤龍香亭。寓意天下大治，國家穩固。
竜の彫刻をほどこした盤竜香亭（香炉の一種）。天下がよく治まり、国が安定しているしるし。

Pavilion-shaped incense holders with coiling-dragon design, indicating great order across the land.

The Hall of Supreme Harmony, the main hall of the three great halls, was designed so that its scale, shape, decoration and furnishings all pointed to the supremacy of imperial authority.

What did a grand ceremony look like? In the Ming Dynasty the Imperial throne, the imperial table, an incense table, musical instruments and guards of honour were prepared well in advance. The emperor would come to the Hall of Supreme Harmony amidst the sound of ceremonial music, drumbeats and firecrackers. He would then sit on the throne to receive obeisances and listen to a reading of congratulatory memorials from his palace courtiers. Then the civil and military officials would all kneel before him and give three cheers of "Long live Your Majesty." Finally the emperor would descend from his throne and go back to the Hall of Canopy (Huagaidian). (The present name, the Hall of Central Harmony, was given in the early Qing Dynasty.) Following Ming tradition with slight modifications, grand ceremonies in the Qing Dynasty remained as elaborate as ever.

The magnificent the interior of the Hall of the Golden Throne. On a platform in the exact centre of the hall stands a golden lacquerware throne carved with coiling dragons, backed by a golden lacquerware dragon screen, and flanked by six pillars entwined with coiling golden dragons. Directly above the throne a huge silver pearl hanges from the mouth of another coiling golden lacquerware dragon.

Officials hardly had a chance to meet the emperor. On grand occasions civil and military officers could only stand in the square in front of the terraces. If one of them was summoned into the emperor's presence in the hall, it was a great honour and favour.

In front of the throne, on both sides, are four pairs of objects, such as mythical birds and animals and ceremonial vessels in ancient style. Incense burners cast in the shape of tripods stand in front of the throne platform. These objects symbolized good luck and longevity.

In front of the Hall of Supreme Harmony were sundials, standard measures, bronze censers, bronze tortoises and bronze cranes, symbolizing the longevity of the emperor and his everlasting power. For grand ceremonies incense would burn in the censers, tortoises and cranes. The spiraling smoke created a solemn and mysterious atmosphere.

To the north of the Hall of Supreme Harmony stand the Hall of Central Harmony and the Hall of Preserving Harmony.

25 鎏金銅缸
鎏金の銅缸
Gilded bronze vat.

26 銅鶴
銅鶴
Bronze crane.

27 日晷
日晷 （日時計）
Sundial.

28 嘉量
嘉量
Standard Measure.

29 銅龜
銅亀
Bronze tortoise.

30 中和殿
　中和殿
　The Hall of Central Harmony.

31 中和殿内景
　中和殿 の内部
　Interior view of the Hall of Central Harmony.

2 夏日
夏の日射し
Summer.

3 保和殿西側
保和殿西側
A back gate of the Hall of Preserving Harmony.

4 三臺
俗に三台と呼ばれる三層の石造基壇
The three layers of white marble that make up the I- shaped terrace.

33

34

35 保和殿內景
保和殿の内部
Interior view of the Hall of Preserving Harmony.

37   36

保和殿後的雲龍大石雕是宮内石雕中最大的。石長十六點五七米，寬三點零七米，厚一點七零米，明代雕造，清乾隆二十六年（一七六一年）重雕。

保和殿の後ろにある雲竜大石刻は、長さ一六・五六メートル、幅三・〇七メートル、厚さ一・七メートル、紫禁城内最大の石刻である。明代につくられたもので、清の乾隆二十六年（一七六一年）に彫りなおされた。

The stone pavement with dra and cloud decoration at the ba the Hall of Preserving Harmony is 1 metres long, 3.07 metres wide and metres thick, the largest carved s in the palace. It was carved in the Dynasty and recarved in 1761, twenty-sixth year of Qing Emp Qianlong's reign.

36 三臺上成排的漢白玉石望柱柱頭
基壇にめぐらした漢白玉欄干柱柱頭
Rows of white marble pillar caps I-shaped terraces.

37 早晨
紫禁城の朝
Morning.

38 保和殿後的雲龍大石雕
保和殿の後ろにある雲竜大石
Carved stone pavement with d and cloud decoration at the ba the Hall of Preserving Harmony.

39　文華殿鳥瞰。清代這裏是舉行經筵及講學的場所。

　文華殿鳥瞰。清代、ここは経書を講義したり、学問を教授する場所であった。
Bird's-eye view of the Hall of Literary Glory, where lectures on philosophy and history were held in the Ming and Qing dynasties.

40　南三所前大影壁
紫禁城最大の、南三所前の目隠し塀
A great screen wall.

41　武英殿鳥瞰。明末農民起義軍領袖李自成曾在這裏登極稱帝，處理政務。

武英殿鳥瞰。明末期の農民蜂起軍の指導者李自成はここで帝位につき、政務をとったことがある。
Bird's-eye view of the Hall of Military Prowess, where Li Zicheng, leader of a peasant uprising in the late Ming Dynasty, ascended the imperial throne and handled government affairs.

文華、武英兩組宮殿爲三大殿的左輔右弼，也屬前朝。東側文華殿、文淵閣在明末曾被火焚毀，康熙年間重建文華殿，又建傳心殿。乾隆年間爲收藏《四庫全書》，將原來位於文華殿南的文淵閣改建在殿北。西側武英殿在清代乾隆年間爲修書印書的地方。同治年間遭火災後重建。武英殿東斷虹橋，保存了明代初建時的風貌。橋北十八槐，係宮中一景。

　文華、武英の両宮殿群は、太和・中和・保和の三大殿の左右にあって、やはり前朝に属している。東側にある文華殿と文淵閣は明末期に焼き払われてしまったが、清の康熙年間に文華殿が再建され、また新しく伝心殿が建てられた。その後、乾隆年間には『四庫全書』を収蔵するため、以前は文華殿の南側にあった文淵閣を文華殿の北側に再建した。西側の武英殿は清の乾隆年間には書物を編纂、印刷する場所であったが、同治年間に火災にあい、再建された。武英殿の東にある断虹橋は明代につくられたが、今でも当時の姿を保ちつづけており、橋の北の十八槐（えんじゅ）は故宮名所の一つになっている。

In the Front Palace two groups of buildings flank the three great halls. On the east are the Hall of Literary Glory (Wenhuadian) and the Imperial Library (Wenyuange), which were destroyed by fire in the late Ming Dynasty. During Qing Emperor Kangxi's reign the Hall of Literary Glory was rebuilt, and at the same time the Hall of Proclaimed Intellect (Chuanxindian) was constructed. To house the Complete Library of the Four Branches of Literature (Sikuquanshu) the Imperial Library, which had been south of the Hall of Literary Glory, was rebuilt to the north of the hall in Emperor Qianlong's reign. On the west is the Hall of Military Prowess (Wuyingdian), which was used for compiling and printing books in the Qianlong period. It was burnt down and rebuilt under the reign of Emperor Tongzhi. Broken Rainbow Bridge (Duanhongqiao) to the east of the Hall of Military Prowess retains the style of the Ming Dynasty, when it was first built. The eighteen Chinese scholartrees north of the bridge form a scenic spot in the Imperial Palace.

43　文淵閣內景
　　文淵閣の内景
　　Interior view of the Imperial Library.

44

45

44
斷虹橋
断虹橋
Broken Rainbow Bridge.

45
斷虹橋倒影
断虹橋の倒影
Broken Rainbow Bridge reflected
in water.

後

三

宮

　從保和殿往北走，經過長方形的乾清門廣場，便到了內廷正門乾清門，門內就是後三宮。

　後三宮（乾清宮、交泰殿和坤寧宮）也座落在＂工＂字形臺基上。後面是御花園（明代稱宮後苑），兩側是東西六宮。俗稱後三宮與東西六宮為＂三宮六院＂。

　保和殿を出て北へ長方形の乾清門広場を横切ると、内廷の正門、乾清門である。門内にあるのが後三宮である。

　後三宮（乾清宮、交泰殿と坤寧宮）も「工」字形の基壇の上に建てられてある。その後ろは御花園（明代には宮後苑と呼ばれた）、両側は東・西六宮である。後三宮と東・西六宮をあわせて、俗に「三宮六院」と呼んでいる。

Walking north from the Hall of Preserving Harmony, one passes a small rectangular square and arrives at the Gate of Heavenly Purity (Qianqingmen), the main entrance to the Inner Palace. Beyond the gate on an I-shaped terrace stand the three rear palaces — the Palace of Heavenly Purity (Qianqinggong), the Hall of Prosperity (Jiaotaidian), and the Hall of Earthly Tranquility (Kunninggong). The three rear Palaces are flanked by the six eastern and six western palaces. These are collectively called Three Palaces and Six Courtyards. To the north of the three rear palaces lies the Imperial Garden.

47
乾清門廣場
乾清門広場
The square in front of the Gate of Heavenly Purity.

48
從保和殿看乾清門
保和殿から見た乾清門
View of the Gate of Heavenly Purity from the Hall of Preserving Harmony.

乾清宮，明代是皇帝的寢宮。嘉靖年間，明帝朱厚熜差一點被宮女楊金英等十餘人在這裏勒死。五十四年之後又發生"紅丸案"，剛繼帝位一個月的朱常洛因吃了"紅丸"，死在宮內。清代順治、康熙兩帝仍住乾清宮，雍正帝以後，乾清宮改為皇帝處理日常政務的場所。殿內"正大光明"匾後，自雍正到道光年間，曾藏放建儲匣，匣內封存皇帝秘密寫定的皇位繼承人，而不公開立太子。

乾清宮は明代では皇帝の寢宮であった。嘉靖年間、明の十一代皇帝朱厚熜は楊金英という宮女たち十余人の手で、ここで首をしめられそうになったことがある。それから54年の後、帝位についてわずか一ヵ月という十四代皇帝朱常洛は「紅丸」を飲んだのがもとで、この宮殿で死んだ。これを「紅丸事件」という。清代には、順治、康熙二帝がやはりここに居住していたが、雍正皇帝以降は日常の政務をみるところとなった。雍正年間から道光年間にかけて、この乾清宮にある「正大光明」と書かれた扁額の後ろには、建儲匣（けんちょばこ）という箱が置かれるようになっていたが、その箱は皇帝がひそかに選んだ次の皇帝繼承者の名を入れておくもので、その間（かん）、立太子は公然となされることはなかった。

乾清宮門額及斗栱
乾清宮の門額とますがた
The signboard and bracketing system of the gate of the Hall of Heavenly Purity.

乾清宮外景
乾清宮外景
Exterior view of the Palace of Heavenly Purity.

In the Ming Dynasty the Palace of Heavenly Purity was the emperor's bedchamber. In 1542 Ming Emperor Jiajing was nearly strangled here by a maid called Yang Jinying and others. Fifty-four years later the "Red Pill Incident" took place here. Emperor Taichang, who had ascended the throne only a month before, died of red pills. The palace remained the emperor's bedchamber during Qing Emperor Shunzhi's time and Kangxi's time. Following Qing Emperor Yongzheng's enthronement the Palace of Heavenly Purity was converted for dealing with routine state affairs. Behind the horizontal board inscribed with four Chinese characters, *"Zheng Da Guang Ming"* (meaning open and above board), above the throne a box for testament on succession to the Qing throne was once cached. It was said that in the reigns of Yongzheng, Qianlong, Jiaqing and Daoguang the emperor's testament regarding his choice of a son as his successor was secreted in this box.

52
乾清宮内寶座
乾清宮内の玉座
The imperial throne
in the Palace of
Heavenly Purity.

53
乾清宮西夾室
乾清宮の西の間
The west gallery of the Palace of Heavenly Purity.

乾清宮後面是交泰殿。清代皇后過生日時，在這裏接受妃嬪、公主、福晉、命婦等人的朝賀。乾隆十一年（1746年）以後，這裏還一直是存放清帝行使權力時使用的二十五顆印璽的地方。

　　乾清宮の後ろにあるのは交泰殿である。清代には、皇后の誕生日祝いともなると、妃嬪、公主、福晋、命婦たちがここに祝賀に参内したものだった。乾隆十一年（1746年）以後になると、ここは清の皇帝が権力を行使するときに使う玉璽、金印二十五個を置いておく場所ともなった。

The Hall of Prosperity (Jiaotaidian) stands to the north of the Palace of Heavenly Purity. On the occasion of her birthday celebration the empress of the Qing Dynasty would come here to accept felicitations from the imperial concubines, princesses, princes' wives, and ladies of rank. Since 1746, the eleventh year of Emperor Qianlong's reign, it has been used for storing twenty-five imperial seals.

54　乾清宮內仙樓　A storied building inside the Palace of Heavenly
　　乾清宮内の仙楼　Purity.

55　交泰殿外景
　　交泰殿外景　　Exterior view of the Hall of Prosperity

56
交泰殿內寶座
交泰殿内の玉座
The throne in the Hall of Prosperity.

58 　交泰殿寶座右側陳設的大自鳴鐘，清嘉慶
三年（1798年）內務府造辦處製造，至今還在
轉動。

交泰殿玉座の右側に置かれている大自鳴鐘。
これは清の嘉慶三年（1798年）、内務府造弁
処でつくったもので、今でも動いている。

The chime clock made in the palace factory in 1798,
the third year of Qing Emperor Jiaqing's reign, was
also kept in the Hall of Prosperity. It still works.

59 　坤寧宮東夾室朱紅金色囍字屏風

坤寧宮の東の間にある朱紅地に双喜の金字を
ほどこした屏風

Vermilion screen with golden "double-happiness"
characters in the east gallery of the Hall of Earthly
Tranquility.

57 　交泰殿內的銅壺滴漏
交泰殿内の銅壺滴漏（水時計）
The copper clepsydra in the Hall of Prosperity.

坤寧宮在明代是皇后居住的正宮。明朝末
代皇帝崇禎的周皇后在這裏自盡。清代這裏名
義上也是皇后的正宮，實際上祇是在大婚時，
皇后和皇帝纔在此宮的東暖閣住三天，此後就
不再啓用了。

坤寧宮は明代には皇后の起居する正宮で
あった。明代最後の崇禎皇帝の后、周皇后は
ここで自殺している。清代になってからも、
名義上ここはやはり皇后の正宮であったが、

実際には婚礼をあげた三日間、皇后と皇帝が
ここの東暖閣に住むだけで、平常は使用しな
かった。

The Hall of Earthly Tranquility (Kunninggong) was
the bedchamber of empresses in the Ming Dynasty.
Empress Zhou of the last Ming emperor, Chongzhen,
committed suicide here. During the Qing Dynasty it
remained in name only as the bedchamber for
empresses; only on the occasion of an imperial wedding did the royal couple stay in the heated east
room of the hall for three days.

61　喜房南沿大炕，皇帝皇后在此飲交杯酒行合卺宴。

新婚部屋南わきのオンドル。皇帝皇后はここで三三九度の盃をとりかわした。

The gorgeous bed in the nuptial chamber where the emperor and empress drank the wedding cup.

63

62　喜牀上掛的五彩百子帳
新婚の寝台にかけられた色とりどりの百子
帳——薄絹に百子図を縫いとったとばり

The coloured curtains of the nuptial bed with the
design of a hundred children playing.

63　坤寧宮内薩満教祭祀場所，這是殺豬煮肉
用的神竈。
坤寧宮内にある薩満教祭祀の場。これは豚
を殺し肉を煮るのに用いる神聖なる竈。

The kitchen range in the Hall of Earthly Tranquility for
cooking pork to offer to the God of Manchu
Lamaism.

御花園

65 堆秀山全景
堆秀山全景
Complete view of the Mountain of Accumulated Refinement (Duixiushan).

建於明代永樂十五年（1417年）的御花園，是自具一格的宮廷式花園，被譽為宮內諸園之首。造園工匠們嫻熟地運用各種技巧，造出了松濤竹影、花木扶疏，既華貴端莊又清幽秀麗的園林風光。園中的欽安殿，是故宮現存最完整的明代建築。

明の永楽十五年（1417年）につくられた御花園は独自の風格をそなえた宮廷式庭園で、紫禁城内第一の庭園でもある。庭師たちは腕によりをかけて、松、竹、花、木の調和をとりながら、高貴、荘厳、加えて閑静、秀麗な庭園風景をつくり出した。庭園内にある欽安殿は、故宮に現存する明代の建物のうち一番完全なものである。

Built in 1417, the fifteenth year of Ming Emperor Yongle's reign, the Imperial Garden has a unique style. Its luxuriant trees and flowers, well spaced, present a beautiful atmosphere of solemnity and dignity. It is considered foremost of the gardens in the palace. The Hall of Imperial Tranquility (Qinandian) in the garden is the most intact Ming building in the Palace Museum.

66

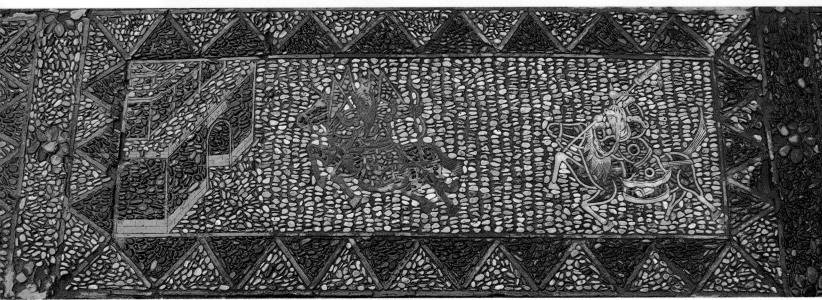
69

70

72 萬春亭
万春亭
Ten Thousand Spring Pavilion (Wanchunting).

73 園内一角
御花園の一角
A corner of the garden.

74 園内龍爪古槐
御花園内の 槐 の老樹
An old Chinese scholartree shaped like a dragon's claw.

御花園的建築保持了宮廷建築左右基本對稱的格局。園內殿亭軒齋高低錯落；古栢蒼松、盆景奇石，遍佈各處。而且園內小徑均用各色卵石鑲拚成戲曲故事、花卉等圖案，另有一番情趣。

御花園の建物は宮廷建築特有の左右対称性という格調を保ちながらも、単調な大同小異という印象を与えないように配慮してある。園内には、楼や亭が各所に散在し、年代のたった松や柏（かしわ）が緑の影をつくり、盆景奇石が庭園のいたるところに配置されている。細い道路には、色や大きさの異なる玉石で、人物、草花などの模様が描きだされていて、何ともいえない格別の雰囲気をかもしだしている。

Even in the Imperial Garden the doctrine of symmetry prevails. Visitors are impressed with the garden's beautiful halls and pavilions, graced by ancient pines and cypresses and jagged rocks in grotesque shapes. The garden paths, with figurative and flower mosaics made of coloured cobbles, enhance one's pleasure in the garden.

78
浮碧亭額匾
浮碧亭の扁額
Inscribed board on the Jade-Green Floating Pavilion (Fubiting).

9 漱芳齋內 " 風雅存 " 小戲臺

漱芳斎の室内にある「風雅存」小舞台

A small theatrical stage called Preservation of Elegance (Fengyacun) in the Lodge of Fresh Fragrance (Soufangzhai).

） 漱芳齋內多寶格

漱芳斎内の飾り棚

The Case of Different Treasures (Duobaoge) in the Lodge of Fresh Fragrance.

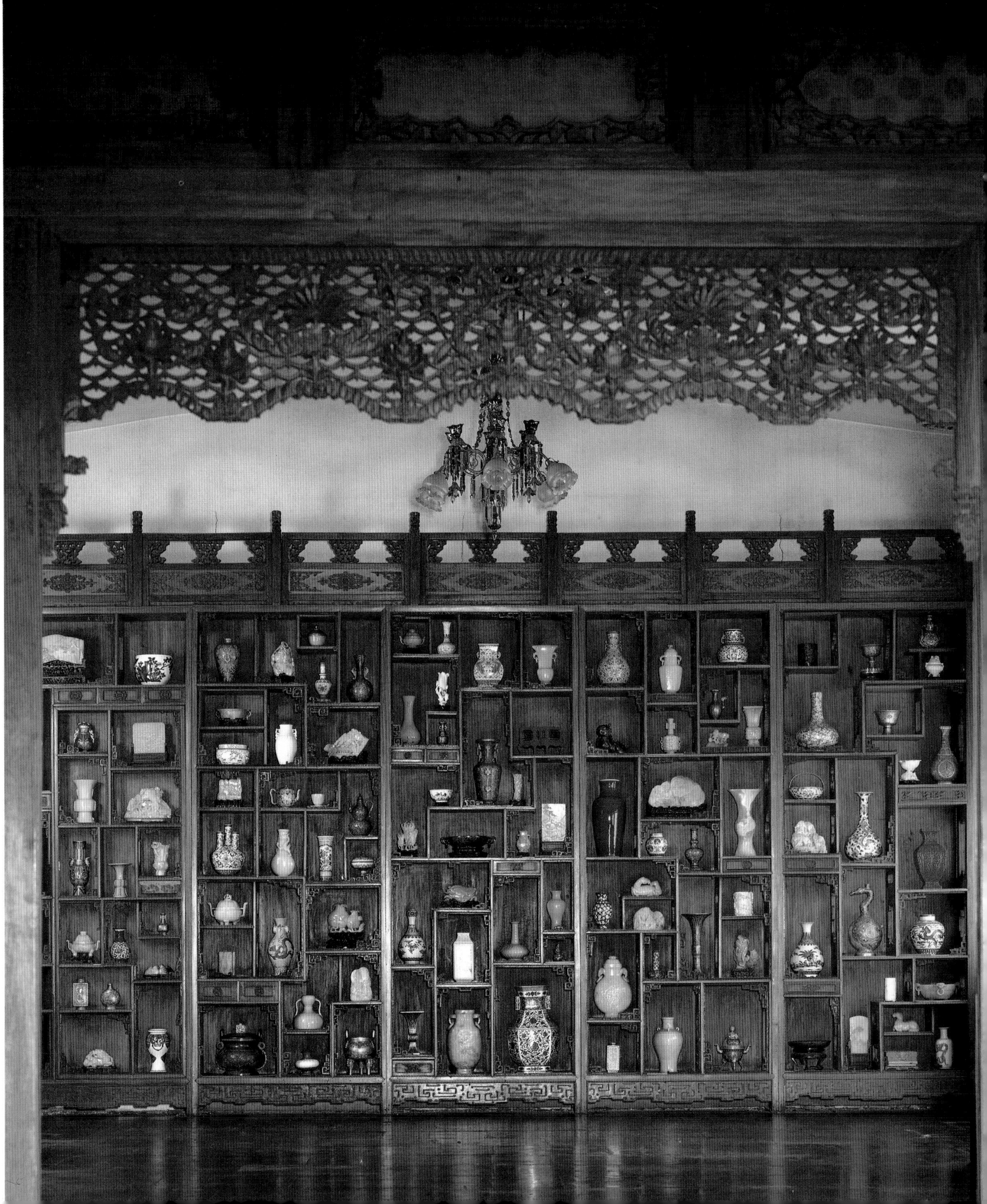

內西路

82
西二長街夜景
西二長街の夜景
Night view of the No. Two long alley to the six western palaces.

内廷の宮殿には、それぞれ深い意味のある名がついている。外朝の宮殿は国を治め、邦を安んじる意味から命栄、賞賛祝福といった意味のものである。

儲秀宮は西六宮のうちの一宮殿で、西太后もここに住み、五十歳の誕生日をむかえたことがある。現在の室内の様子は、その時の模様を記した宮殿記録にもとづいて、調度品などを選び、陳列したものである。

內廷各殿命名均有深義,各有所指,諸如表示妻道之禮,寓意後昆蕃衍,歌頌祝福之詞等,與外朝各殿標榜治國安邦的命名不同。

儲秀宮是西六宮之一,慈禧太后曾在這裏居住,度過五十壽誕。如今室內布置是按慈禧做壽時的宮廷陳設檔案陳列的。

The names of halls or palaces in the Inner Palace had profound implications, such as female virtues, multiplication of descendants and good wishes, whereas those in the Front Palace claimed good administration of the country.
The Palace of Concentrated Beauty (Chuxiugong) is one of the six western palaces. Empress Dowager Cixi once lived here. Now the furnishings in the room are all arranged as they were on the occasion of Cixi's fiftieth birthday celebration.

83

儲秀宮外景
儲秀宮の外景
...terior view of the Palace of Concentrated Beauty.

...秀宮内 · 角
...秀宮 の内部
... corner of the interior of the palace of Concen-
...ted Beauty.

儲秀宮於明永樂十八年（1420年）建成，原名壽昌宮，嘉靖十四年（1535年）改今名。清代曾多次修葺，最大的一次修葺在光緒十年（1884年）。這年十月十日是慈禧的五十生辰，在這裏舉辦慶祝活動，她同時移居此宮。這次修建，共耗費白銀六十三萬両之多。在庭院內鑄造了一對戲珠銅龍和一對銅梅花鹿，重施建築彩畫，重掛聯匾，重新裝修雕花紫檀木落地罩和雕花楠木門窗，紋飾內容多與祝壽有關。院內廊壁上也刻滿了大臣為慈禧祝壽的頌詞。

儲秀宮室內裝修豪華精美。慈禧的臥室在西里間，也叫西暖閣，外邊是西次間，中間用花梨木雕的萬福萬壽邊框鑲的大玻璃作隔斷。身在暖閣，可以隔着玻璃看見次間的一切，既隔斷而又未隔斷，這在紫禁城內是僅有的巧妙構思。

儲秀宮は明の永楽十八年（1420年）に建てられたもので、もとの名を寿昌宮といい、嘉靖十四年（1535年）に現在の名に改称された。清代になってから何度も改装されているが、一番大がかりだったのは光緒十年（1884年）の時である。それはこの年の十月十日が西太后の五十歳誕生日で、ここで祝賀の行事をおこない、またここに住むことになったからである。この改装には白銀六十三万両を投じたということである。庭には珠とたわむれる銅製の竜一対、銅鹿一対がすえられ、建物に

は新しく色彩が加えられた。また、対句になった額、彫刻をほどこした紫檀の花台、同じく彫刻をほどこした楠の窓枠などいずれも新しく改装され、模様や飾りは長寿を祝うものとなった。庭の回廊の壁にも、西太后の誕生五十歳を祝う大臣たちの賛辞をあたりいっぱいに彫刻した。

儲秀宮の室内装飾はたいへん豪華なものである。西太后の寝室は西側の奥の間で、西暖閣ともいうが、西の脇の間とは「万福万寿」の字を彫刻したカリンの木枠をつけた大きなガラスでへだてられている。身は西暖閣に居ながら脇の間の様子が一目瞭然というわけである。遮断されているようで、遮断されていない。こうした効果は広い紫禁城内でもここだけで、当時はたいへん珍しいものだった。

The Palace of Concentrated Beauty was built in 1420, the eighteenth year of Ming Emperor Yongle's reign. It was formerly named the Palace of Longevity and Prosperity (Shouchanggong) and in 1535, the fourteenth year of Ming Emperor Jiajing's reign, was given its present name. During the Qing Dynasty the palace was repaired many times. In 1884, the tenth year of Emperor Guangxu's reign, it received its largest renovation. On October 10 the same year Empress Dowager Cixi's fiftieth birthday was celebrated here, and, at the same time, Cixi moved her residence into the palace. The renovation cost 630,000 taels of silver. A pair of bronze dragons playing with pearls and a pair of sikas were cast and placed in the courtyard, coloured images of the palace were repainted, new horizontal tablets and vertical couplets replaced old ones, carved red sandal wood partitions and carved *nanmu* doors and windows were renewed. Most of the patterns were connected with birthday celebrations, and the corridor walls in the courtyard were full of courtiers' congratulations on Cixi's birthday.

The interior decorations were luxurious and beautiful. The heated west room of the palace was used as Cixi's bedchamber, separated from the next room by a glass partition with rosewood frame carved with characters meaning fortune and longevity. Through this glass partition everything in the next room could be seen clearly. This sort of quasi-partition was the only one in the Forbidden City and considered an innovation at the time.

86

87

85

儲秀宮內正間原懸有乾隆帝御書"茂修內治"匾，慈禧換掛"大圓寶鏡"匾。

儲秀宮の正面の間には、もとは「茂修内治」と書いた乾隆皇帝直筆の扁額がかかっていたが、西太后はこれをも「大圓宝鏡」の扁額にかけかえた。

The main room of the Palace of Concentrated Beauty originally had a horizontal tablet with Chinese characters meaning self-culture and self-control, written by Emperor Qianlong, but Cixi used a new tablet with her characters, meaning a large round mirror in place of the old.

86、87
儲秀宮內擺設
儲秀宮内部の様子
Artware in the Palace of Concentrated Beauty.

88、89
儲秀宮內陳設
儲秀宮内部の様子
Furnishings in the Palace of Concentrated Beauty.

90　92
儲秀宮院內廂房額匾
儲秀宮中庭の左右両側建物の扁額
A horizontal inscribed board in the wing of the Palace of Concentrated Beauty.

91
體和殿北額匾
体和殿の北の扁額
A horizontal inscribed board in the Hall of Manifest Harmony (Tihedian).

93　長春宮東次間

　　長春宮の東の脇の間

　　A room in the Palace of Eternal Spring.

94　從長春宮院內戲臺看長春宮

　　長春宮の中庭にある舞台から見た長春宮

　　The Palace of Eternal Spring seen from the stage in its
　　courtyard.

95　典雅工細、融合西洋透視方法繪成的長春

　　宮《紅樓夢》壁畫局部

　　洋式の遠近法をもとりいれて緻密に優美に描

　　かれた長春宮の『紅楼夢』壁画の部分

　　Part of the wall painting illustrating the famous
　　Chinese novel *A Dream of Red Mansions*. Drawn in
　　perspective and with close attention to detail, the
　　painting is elegant.

長春宮爲西六宮之一，明代天啓帝的李妃居住過。清同治帝親政後，慈禧太后從養心殿移居住過這裏。光緒帝之妃和遜帝溥儀之妾也都在這裏住過。院內戲臺於嘉慶十五年（一八一〇年）改建，慈禧住在長春宮時，常在這裏戲。

長春宮四周走廊內，繪有十幾巨幅《紅樓夢》壁畫。其中一幅描繪的是賈母遊園的情景，正是西太后「時以賈太君自擬」的旁證。這些壁畫大約作於光緒年間瑾、珍二妃命畫苑繪《大觀園圖》的同一時代。

長春宮は西六宮のうちの一宮殿で、明代に
は天啓皇帝の李妃が住んだことがある。清の
同治皇帝の李妃が位につくと、西太后も養心殿
からここに移った。光緒皇帝や最後の皇帝溥儀の
妃もここに住んだことがある。中庭には嘉慶
十五年（一八一〇年）に改築された舞台もあ
り、西太后が長春宮に住んでいたときには、
よくここで芝居を見たものである。

長春宮の周囲の回廊には、小説『紅楼夢』
の大きな壁画が十数幅もえがかれている。そ
のなかには、賈母遊園の場面があるが、これ
は西太后が「時に賈太君をもって、自らを
擬え」たしるしではないだろうか。これら
の壁画は光緒年間のもので、瑾妃、珍妃の二
人が画苑に命じてえがかせた『大観園図』と
同じ時代にあたるものである。

96　長春宮妃嬪卧室

長春宮の妃嬪の寝室

Bedchamber for concubines in the Palace of Eternal Spring.

The Palace of Eternal Spring (Changchungong), one of the six western palaces, was used as a residence by the concubine Li of Emperor Tianqi of the Ming Dynasty. After Emperor Tongzhi of the Qing Dynasty took over the reign, Empress Dowager Cixi moved her residence from the Hall of Mental Cultivation (Yangxindian) to this palace. The concubines of the emperors Guangxu and Xuantong once also lived here. The stage in the courtyard was rebuilt in 1810, the fifteenth year of Emperor Jiaqing's reign. Cixi often watched theatrical performances here while living in the Palace of Eternal Spring.

On the walls of the corridors around the palace are more than ten large paintings illustrating the *A Dream of Red Mansions*, a famous Chinese novel. One painting depicted Lady Dowager Jia touring a garden. This is circumstantial evidence for the fact that Empress Dowager Cixi always likened herself to Lady Dowager Jia in the novel. These wall paintings were made in approximately the same period that the concubines Jin and Zhen, during the reign of Emperor Guangxu, ordered the court artists to paint the Grand View Garden (Daguanyuan).

97
太極殿內景之一
太極殿内部、その一
Part of the interior of the Hall of Great Supremacy.

東西六宮的建築左右對稱，格局基本相同，都是一座座正方形的院落，院門居中，各有前後兩座殿宇及兩廂配殿，組合成兩進三合院。目前西六宮室內尚保持后妃居住時的原狀。

太極殿爲西六宮之一，明代初名未央宮。嘉靖十四年（1535年）改名啓祥宮。清康熙年間重建以後，改稱太極殿。清同治帝的瑜妃曾在這裏居住。

東・西六宮の建物はだいたい同じ格式で、いずれも正方形の敷地に、左右対称の作りでできている。門をくぐって中に入れば、前後二棟の建物にそれぞれ左右二棟の配殿が組み合わされていて、三つの中庭を形づくっている。西六宮の室内は、今でも皇后・妃嬪たちの住んでいた頃のままの状態に保たれている。

太極殿は西六宮の一宮殿で、明初期には未央宮といっていたが、嘉靖十四年（1535年）に、啓祥宮と改名された。清の康熙年間に新たに改築されたのち、今の太極殿という名になった。清の同治皇帝の瑜妃もここに住んだことがある。

The six eastern palaces and the six western palaces are symmetrical. Square in shape, each palace unit is a compound with the door in the middle of the front wall. The compound is divided into two courtyards, each containing one main hall. In addition, there are two wings in one compound. Now all the furnishings in the six western palaces remain as they were when the empresses and imperial concubines of the Ming and Qing dynasties lived there.

The Hall of Great Supremacy (Taijidian), one of the six western palaces, was called Palace of Endlessness (Weiyanggong) in the early Ming Dynasty and renamed Palace of Blessings (Qixiangong) in 1535, the fourteenth year of Ming Emperor Jiajing's reign. It was rebuilt and received its present name in the reign of Qing Emperor Kangxi. Concubine Yu of Qing Emperor Tongzhi once lived here.

建於清乾隆年間的雨花閣，位於慈寧宮北春華門內，是宮中喇嘛教建築。三層樓閣，鎏金銅瓦，造型別致。

皇宮內有許多殿閣專供祭祀活動之用，遺留至今的有明代的道教神殿，清代的佛堂，祀孔祭祖以及皇帝祭祀壇廟前齋戒用的宮殿等。

過世皇帝的遺孀，即太后太妃們居住的慈寧宮、壽安宮、壽康宮等區，佛堂最多。

清の乾隆年間に建てらてた雨花閣は、故宮におけるラマ教建築物で、慈寧宮北の春華門内にある。三重の楼閣で、屋根瓦は特殊な方法でつくった鎏金（金メッキ）の銅瓦を使い、格別な趣きの造型をもっている。

皇宮にはもっぱら祭祀に使う建物もたくさんある。今も残っているものでは、明代の道教神殿、清代の仏堂、孔子や祖先をまつったり、皇帝が祭祀をする前に斎戒に使った宮殿などがある。

皇帝が世を去って残された太后や太妃たちが住む慈寧宮、寿安宮、寿康宮などの区画には、仏堂が一番多い。

Built in Qing Emperor Qianlong's period, the Pavilion of the Rain of Flowers (Yuhuage) is situated inside Spring of Flower Gate (Chunhuamen), north of the Palace of Benevolent Peace (Cininggong). This pavilion, a three-storied building with gilt bronze tiles, is unique in Lamaist architecture.

In the imperial palace many halls and pavilions served exclusively as places for offering sacrifices to the gods. Existing buildings include the Ming temple for offering sacrifices to the Taoist God, the Qing hall for worshipping Buddha, and the hall for the emperor's fast before offering sacrifices.

Most of the Buddhist temples were located in the Palace of Benevolent Peace, the Palace of Peace and Longevity (Shouangong) and the Palace of Longevity and Health (Shoukanggong), the quarters of the empresses dowager and dowager secondary-consorts.

98
太極殿內景之二
太極殿内部、その二
Part of the interior of the Hall of Great Supremacy.

99
雨花閣外景
雨花閣の外景
Exterior view of the Pavilion of the Rain of Flowers.

00 慈寧花園咸若館內佛龕一角
　　慈寧花園の咸若館内の仏龕

A corner of a shrine in the Hall of All Peace in the Garden of Benevolent Peace.

慈寧花園中的慈蔭樓、寶相樓、吉雲樓、咸若館、臨溪亭等都是佛堂。

慈寧花園内にある慈蔭楼、宝相楼、吉雲楼、咸若館、臨渓亭などは、いずれも仏堂である。

The main buildings in the Garden of Benevolent Peace (Cining Huayuan) were Buddhist temples, such as the Hall of Immeasurable Kindness and Mercy (Ciyinlou), the Building for Images of Buddhas (Baoxianglou), the Hall of Auspicious Clouds (Jiyunlou), the Hall of All Peace (Xianruoguan) and the Pavilion over a Pond (Linxiting).

101
英華殿院內的菩提樹
英華殿の庭にある菩提樹
Pipal tree in the garden of the Hall of Flowers (Yinghuachan).

102
菩提樹葉子上繪製的佛教人物畫
菩提樹の葉にえがかれた仏教人物画
Buddhist figures painted on a pipal leaf.

養心殿

紫禁城宮殿建築羣中，除前三殿後三宮外，最引人注目的當首推養心殿了。養心殿位於後三宮西南，北接西六宮，軍機處近在咫尺，是雍正帝以後清代各帝處理政務、發號施令的地方。

養心殿建於明朝，清雍正年間重修。自雍正帝以後到清末，清帝多在這裏居住，有好幾個皇帝死在這裏。慈禧太后曾在這裏垂簾聽政，清帝宣統的退位詔書也是在這裏簽署的。

養心殿共有兩個院落。建築本身為"工"字形建築，佈局得體。前殿端莊實用，宜於辦事；後殿幽深恬靜，適合就寢。廊廡環抱，並建有多種附屬用房。

紫禁城のなかにある宮殿建築群のうち、前三殿後三宮を除けば、一番人目をひくのは養心殿である。養心殿は後三宮の西南にあり、北は西六宮と接している。軍機処がすぐ近くにあって、雍正皇帝以後は清代各皇帝が政務をとり、号令を発する所となっていた。

養心殿は明代につくられた後、清の雍正年間に改築されている。雍正皇帝の頃から清末期にいたるまで、清の皇帝のほとんどはここに住み、また何人もの皇帝がここで死んでいる。西太后もここで「垂簾の政」（簾をおろして政務をとるの意）をおこなったし、また、宣統皇帝溥儀もここで「退位詔書」に署名した。

養心殿は前後二つの宮殿からなり、建物自身は「工」字形建築物で、非常に手際よく配置されている。前殿は政務をとるのにふさわしいように、荘重に実用的になっており、後殿は就寝に適するように、静かで奥まった感じになっている。これを中心に廊下がめぐり、多種多用の付属的建物がたくさん建てられてある。

A place deserving special mention is the Hall of Mental Cultivation (Yangxindian). It stands southwest of the three rear palaces and south of the six western palaces, close to the Office of Grand Council of State. The Qing emperors, beginning with Yongzheng, handled routine affairs and issued orders here.

The hall was built in the Ming Dynasty and repaired under Qing Emperor Yongzheng's reign. From Yongzheng's reign to the end of the Qing Dynasty most of the Qing emperors lived here. A number of them died here. It was also here that Empress Dowager Cixi ruled the country from behind a screen and Qing Emperor Xuantong signed the imperial edict of abdication after the Revolution of 1911.

I-shaped, the hall has a good layout. It contains two large courtyards with galleries and subsidiary rooms suitable for various purposes. Dignified and practical, the front hall was good for conducting daily government activities. The rear hall, in the quiet surroundings, was a good place for rest.

106

104

養心殿鳥瞰

養心殿鳥瞰

Bird's-eye view of the Hall of Mental Cultivation.

105

從玉壁中心洞眼看養心門匾額

玉壁の中心孔から養心門の扁額をのぞく

Inscribed plaque of the Gate of Mental Cultivation seen through a hole in the centre of the jade tablet.

106

養心殿正間寶座，是皇帝接見大臣的地方。

養心殿正面の間の玉座。ここは皇帝が大臣を

接見するところであった。

Imperial throne in the main room of the Hall of Mental Cultivation. Here the emperor gave audience to his ministers.

107　養心殿東暖閣兩重寶座——慈禧垂簾聽政處
養心殿東暖閣の二重の玉座——西太后が「垂
簾の政」をおこなった場所。
The two thrones in the heated east room of the Hall of
Mental Cultivation.

養心殿東暖閣室內採光充分，進門處空間較大，迎門面西背東設兩重寶座，以黃紗簾相隔。慈禧垂簾聽政時，小皇帝坐前，慈禧坐後，如今的陳設仍是當年的原狀。

養心殿西暖閣，是皇帝批閱奏章和與要臣親信面授機密的地方，環境隱蔽。相連的西側小間就是著名的三希堂，因乾隆帝在這裏收藏稀世法書《快雪時晴帖》、《中秋帖》和《伯遠帖》而得名。

養心殿後殿共五間，不另設門，安寧舒適。東西兩梢間各設龍牀。連接前後殿的穿堂短廊，東西各有一門。東面的體順堂是皇后侍寢的臨時寢宮，西面的燕禧堂是妃嬪聽候召喚的居室。

108
養心殿內三希堂
養心殿内の三希堂
Room of Three Rarities in the Hall of
Mental Cultivation.

養心殿の東暖閣には明りが十分に入れるようになっている。門を入ったところには大きくゆとりがとってあり、正面に西向きの玉座が二つ前後に並んでいる。二つの玉座は黄色い薄絹の簾で区切られるようになっていて、西太后が「垂簾の政」をみたときには、幼い皇帝が前の玉座に坐り、西太后が後ろの玉座に坐っていた。今の配置はその頃の配置そのままである。

養心殿の西暖閣は、皇帝が上奏文書を決裁し、重臣や腹心のものと協議したりする場所で、それにふさわしいつくりになっている。これにつづく西側の小さな部屋が有名な三希堂で、乾隆皇帝が『快雪時晴帖』、『中秋帖』、『伯遠帖』など世に希な書道の本を収蔵していたことからこの名を得ている。

養心殿の後殿はあわせて五部屋あるが、表に通じる余計な門はつくっていないので、安静で住みやすいようになっている。東西両端の間にはそれぞれ皇帝の寝台がある。前後二殿をつなぐ渡り廊下には、東西両側にそれぞれ門が一つずつついている。東側の体順堂は皇后が皇帝と寝を共にするときの臨時の寝宮であり、西側の燕禧堂は妃嬪たちが声のかかるのを待つ部屋である。

The heated east room of the Hall of Mental Cultivation receives full natural lighting. Here Empress Dowager Cixi ruled the country from behind a screen. The two thrones in this room were separated by a curtain of yellow gauze. The front throne was for the infant emperor and the one behind the curtain for the Empress Dowager. They are arranged as they were.

The heated west room was the emperor's office, in which he read memorandums and reports, issued orders and held private audiences with trusted followers. The suite west of this room is the famous Room of Three Rarities (Sanxitang), so called because Qing Emperor Qianlong kept here three rare pieces of calligraphy — "Clear Sky After Pleasant Snow," "Mid-Autumn" and "Bo Yuan."

Behind the main hall is a rear hall partitioned into five quiet, comfortable rooms. Beds were placed in the room at the east and west ends. Linking the front and the rear is a short covered passage with two doors, one facing east and the other west. The Hall of State Satisfaction (Tishuntang) in the east was the antechamber used by the empress while waiting for the emperor, and the western wing — the Hall of Peace and Happiness (Yanxitang) — was used as sleeping quarters for the imperial concubines waiting for the emperor's call at night.

皇帝龍牀
皇帝の寝台
Bed for the emperor.

112　養心殿天花正中的渾金蟠龍藻井
　　　養心殿天井の真中にある、金の蟠竜を描いた
　　　藻井（装飾天井）
　　　A coiling golden dragon on the ceiling of the Hall of
　　　Mental Cultivation.

外東路

114
從皇極門內呑九龍壁
皇極門内から九竜壁をのぞむ
View of Nine-Dragon Wall from inside the Gate of Ultimate Greatness.

115
寧壽門匾額
寧寿門の扁額
Horizontal inscribed board on the Gate of Peaceful Longevity.

寧壽宮位於紫禁城內東北隅，今繪畫館、珍寶館所在地。原是明代仁壽宮與噦鸞諸宮，為宮妃養老之所。清康熙年間改稱寧壽宮，為東朝太后住處。乾隆三十六年（1771年）至四十一年（1776年）改建，共耗銀一百四十三萬餘兩之多，目的是供乾隆帝執政六十年歸政後做太上皇時享用。

寧壽宮仿大內中軸綫上的宮殿，即前朝後寢的格式修建，大體分前後兩部份。皇極殿、寧壽宮既是全宮又是前半部的主體，皇極門、寧壽門庭院間，點植蒼松，環境幽美。後半部分三路，中路為養性殿、樂壽堂和頤和軒。養性殿制如養心殿，樂壽堂亦稱讀書堂。

116

116 寧壽門外景
寧寿門の外景
Exterior view of the Gate of Peaceful Longevity.

117 寧壽門前鎏金銅獅
寧寿門前の鎏金銅獅子
Gilt bronze lion in front of the Gate of Peaceful Longevity.

寧寿宮は紫禁城内の東北隅にあって、今は
絵画館と珍宝館になっている。明代には仁寿
宮、噦鸞諸宮といって、宮妃たちの養老の場
所であったが、清の康熙年間に寧寿宮と改め
られ、皇太后の住まいとなった。乾隆三十六
年から四十一年（1771～1776年）にかけて、
銀百四十三万余両を費やして改築されたが、
それは乾隆皇帝が60年間執政して太上皇に
なった時に使用するためであった。

寧寿宮は、故宮中軸線上の宮殿を模して、

前半部は政治用、後半部は住居用という形式
で建てられ、だいたい前後二つの部分にわけ
られる。皇極殿、寧寿宮は寧寿宮宮殿群全体
の、また前半部の主体ともなっている。皇極
門と寧寿門との間の庭には緑の松が点在し、
美しく、静かな雰囲気がたちこめている。後
半部は三路にわけられる。中路は養性殿、楽
寿堂と頤和軒で、養性殿は養心殿にならって
つくられており、楽寿堂は読書堂とも呼ばれ
ている。

Located in the northeastern corner of the Forbidden City is the Complex of Peaceful Longevity (Ningshougong), where the House of Paintings and the Treasure Houses are today. Originally called the Palace of Benevolence and Longevity (Renshougong) and used as living quarters for older imperial concubines in the Ming Dynasty, this group of buildings was renamed the Palace of Peaceful Longevity under Qing Emperor Kangxi's reign and changed into living quarters for the Empress Dowager. Between 1771 and 1776 (thirty-sixth to forty-first year of Qing Emperor Qianlong's reign), Emperor Qianlong spent more than 1,430,000 taels of silver to rebuild the palace for his own use after abdicating in favour of his son after ruling for sixty years.

This complex is roughly divided into two parts, following the pattern of the Front Palace and the Inner palace on the axis, namely, the front part for conducting state affairs, the rear part for imperial rest. The Hall of Ultimate Greatness (Huangjidian) and the Palace of Peaceful Longevity (Ningshougong) are the main buildings not only of the front part but also of the whole complex. Dotted with green pines, the courtyard between the Gate of Ultimate Greatness (Huangjimen) and the Gate of Peaceful Longevity (Ningshoumen) is picturesque. The rear part is divided into three sections. The Hall of Character Cultivation (Yangxindian), the Hall of Delighted Longevity (Leshoutang) and the Hall of Peace and Rest (Yihexuan) are located in the middle. The Hall of Character Cultivation was modelled after the Hall of Mental Cultivation and the Hall of Delighted Longevity was also called the Reading Room.

118 九龍壁局部
九竜壁（部分）
Part of the Nine-Dragon Wall.

119 在紫禁城城墙上看皇极殿
紫禁城の城壁上から見た皇極殿
The Hall of Ultimate Greatness seen from the wall of the Forbidden City.

皇帝和宮眷大多喜歡聽戲。皇宮內戲臺很多，大都分佈在內廷區。這些戲臺有大有小，有室內也有室外，適應不同規模的演出。寧壽宮後半部東路的暢音閣戲樓，為故宮內最高大的一座三重崇樓，由上至下稱福臺、祿臺、壽臺，臺下地下室有窨井五眼，以供演戲時產生共鳴效果。

皇帝とその眷属は芝居を見るのが好きで、そのため、紫禁城内には舞台がたくさんつくられた。大部分は内廷にあって、大小さまざま、屋内のもあれば、屋外のもあるので、どのような芝居でもどこかで演じることができた。寧寿宮後半部の東路にある暢音閣戯楼は、故宮最大の三階式舞台で、上から下へ福台、禄台、寿台という名がついている。上演のときに共鳴の効果をえるようにと、その奈落には五つのマンホールがつくられてある。

暢音閣

導和怡泰

壼天宣豫

120 暢音閣大戲臺外景
　　暢音閣大舞台の外景
　　Exterior view of the Pavilion of Pleasant Sounds.

121 暢音閣三層崇樓外景
　　三階建楼閣の暢音閣
　　Exterior view of the three-storied Pavilion of Pleasant
　　Sounds.

Most of the emperors and their families were fond of opera. A large number of stages were to be found in the Inner Palace — large and small, indoor and outdoor, to suit different purposes. In the eastern section of the rear part of the Palace of Peaceful Longevity there is a three-storied building named Pavilion of Pleasant Sounds (Changyinge), the largest of its kind in the imperial palace. There is a stage on every level, from top to bottom: Stage of Fortune (Futai), Stage of Prosperity (Lutai), and Stage of Longevity (Shoutai). Five wells in the room below were used to produce sound effects during a performance.

122

122
暢音閣中層內景
暢音閣二階—禄台の内部
Interior of the middle Stage of Prosperity.

123
暢音閣上層內景
暢音閣三階—福台の内部
Interior of the top floor of the Pavilion of Pleasant Sounds.

124 寧壽宮花園禊賞亭內的流盃渠

寧寿宮花園の禊賞亭内の流杯渠 <ruby>流杯渠<rt>りゅうはいきょ</rt></ruby>

Cup-Floating Stream in the Pavilion of the Ceremony of Purification in the Garden of the Palace of Peaceful Longevity.

125　寧壽宮花園內聳秀亭
　　　寧寿宮花園内の聳秀亭
**The Pavilion of Towering Beauty in the Garden of the
Palace of Peaceful Longevity.**

126 聳秀亭抹角樑架
　　聳秀亭の桁構
**Roof-beam structure of the Pavilion of Towering
Beauty.**

寧壽宮後半部西路是寧壽宮花園，南北縱深160餘米，橫廣約37米，在窄長如帶的地域內，造出了布局緊湊靈活、空間時閉時暢、曲直相間、虛實相生、氣氛諧調的園林。

全園大致分四個段落，南自衍祺門而入，古華軒坐中，山石亭臺，林木森隆，為全園最佳景致。進而為遂初堂四合院、粹賞樓。再往後為符望閣，是園中的主體建築。

園內共有建築物二十餘座，大小相襯，上下相錯，靈巧新穎，有別於方圓規矩的宮殿模式。

園內山石亭景，別具風采；峰巒成羣，崖壁陡峭，洞壑幽邃，美不勝收。

寧寿宮後半部の西路は寧寿宮花園で、南北に伸び、長さは百六十余メートル、幅は約三十七メートルである。この帯のような細長い土地に、変化に満ちながら、なお調和のとれた庭園が配置されている。

この庭園はだいたい四つのブロックにわけられる。南から衍祺門をくぐれば、中央に座した古華軒に出る。築山、奇岩、亭に台、木々は緑の繁みをつくる。名勝もかくやと思うばかりで、全園第一の佳景である。歩をすすめれば、遂初堂四合院、粋賞楼とつづく。さらに行けば、寧寿宮花園の中心ともいえる建築物——符望閣に達する。

寧寿宮花園には、二十あまりの建物があるが、大小、上下と調和をとりながら、それぞれ巧みに工夫がこらされており、方円をきまりとする宮殿形式とは異なっている。

寧寿宮花園の風景は、また格別である。園内に一歩足をふみいれれば、山また山、高い崖を行くかと思えば、いつのまにか幽谷に足をふみいれている。その変化と美しさの妙は筆につくしえない。

In the western rear part of the Palace of Peaceful Longevity is the Garden of the Palace of Peaceful Longevity. It covers a long, narrow area of 160 metres from north to south and 37 metres from east to west. The layout of the garden alternates space with mass and curves with straight lines to achieve both unity and harmony. This garden may be divided into four scenic spots. Entering the Gate of Spreading Happiness (Yanqimen), one first sees the Pavilion of Ancient Flowers (Guhuaxuan), which is surrounded by dense trees, rockeries and terraces and presents a particularly beautiful view. Next are a quadrangle named the Hall of Wish Fulfilment (Suichutang) and the Building for Viewing Beautiful Scenery (Cuishanglou). Finally, the Pavilion for Good Wishes (Fuwangge), a magnificent two-storied building, is the major building in the garden.

More than twenty buildings of different sizes, shapes and character decorate the garden, all different from the regular palaces in style.

The garden is also noted for its beautifully arranged rockery.

127 碧螺亭，圖案全用梅花，仿佛無數梅花簇擁的一隻大花籃，色彩豐富，俗稱梅花亭。

碧螺亭は梅の花かごともいえる。数知れない梅の花を図案としており、その色彩の豊かさは格別で、普通、梅花亭といわれている。

The Pavilion of Jade-Green Conch Shell (Biluoting), is also known as the Pavilion of Plum Blossoms. All the decorative motifs and colours are suggestive of plum blossoms, so the pavilion looks like a large basket of flowers.

128
倦勤齋室內小戲臺
倦勤斎の室内小舞台
A small stage in the Lodge for Retired Life

倦勤齋是寧壽宮花園最北端的一座建築物。正中前檐下懸乾隆御筆"倦勤齋"額，取"耄期倦於勤"之意，顯示這裏是太上皇的憩息之所。從布局藝術來說，符望閣是全園的高潮，倦勤齋則如後罩房。室內嵌竹絲掛檐，鑲玉透綉槅扇，一派江南景色，精緻絕倫。

倦勤斎は寧壽花園宮最北端の建物である。正面の軒先には、乾隆皇帝直筆の「倦勤斎」という額がかかっている。意味は「老いて勤に倦む」で、ここが乾隆帝だった太上皇の憩いの場であることを示している。庭園の配置芸術という点からいえば、符望閣はこの庭園全体の最重点であり、倦勤斎はその後ろの付属的建物のようである。倦勤斎の室内には竹ひごを嵌めこんだ楣飾り、玉象嵌や刺しゅうのある仕切りなどがあり、一面に江南地方の風景をとりいれた造作は、まことに巧みである。

The Lodge for Retired Life (Juanqinzhai) is the northernmost building in the Garden of the Palace of peaceful Longevity (Ningshougong Garden). The tablet over the front gate, inscribed with the characters *"Juan Qin Zhai,"* written by Emperor Qianlong, shows that it was the retirement home of the emperor's father. Its furnishings, modelled after articles made in places south of the Yangtze River, are exquisite.

129 從如亭漏窗看符望閣

如亭の花窓から符望閣をのぞむ

The Pavilion for Good Wishes seen from a window in
the Ru Ting Pavilion.

130 如亭

寧寿宮花園内の如亭

Ru Ting Pavilion.

132
倦勤齋室內一角
倦勤斎の室内
A corner of the lodge.

133
倦勤齋正間寶座
倦勤斎正面の間の玉座
The imperial throne in the main room of the Lodge for Retired Life.

135 寧壽宮西夾道
寧寿宮の西夾道
The long western alley of the Palace of Peaceful Longevity.

後記

本圖册由故宮博物院紫禁城出版社編輯出版，系統、扼要、形象地反映了明清兩代皇宮——紫禁城的當今風貌。

本圖册的照片，主要由胡錘先生拍攝；另外選用了方振寧、宗同昌兩位先生的作品；還有曾年、于云天、張曉巍、林京、狄源滄、歐志培、楊茵諸先生的作品。中文說明由汪萊茵女士撰寫，劉北汜先生審定。日文譯者爲邱茂先生，並由林台先生校定。英文譯者、美國專家Marcia Marx女士和湯博文先生校譯。此外，還要感謝北京外文出版社日、英文部其他先生、女士的協助。

《紫禁城》圖册是在故宮博物院領導提議、支持下，由肖政文、劉北汜、吳建羣先生最初參與規劃，經過紫禁城出版社工作人員努力配合下完成的。編排、美術設計是方振寧先生。

本册所刊廣告，除我院合作夥伴——香港商務印書館的壹幀外，其它均由日本國際通訊社總經理黃遠竹先生協助聯系，香港建義利有限公司董事長、總經理田益民先生爲本圖册的印製給予協助，特此一併鳴謝。

故宮博物院
紫禁城出版社社長
李毅華　謹啓
一九八六年十一月

紫禁城

編輯出版　紫禁城出版社（北京故宮博物院內）
印　　刷　凸版印刷（新加坡）有限公司
承　　印　建義利有限公司
發　　行　紫禁城出版社
版　　次　一九八七年一月第一版第一次印刷
統一書號　8314·068
國際書號　ISBN 7-80047-004-0

Seiko creates
new elegance,
apparent as the time.

Beyond the rare beauty of detail there is an innate
elegance, a peerless quality of finish that enriches
every design in the new Seiko collection for men and
women. It is an apt reflection of the extraordinary
technology within.

精工表婀娜典雅
显示着永恒的时时刻刻

造型精美典雅，走时准确无双，每个新
姿态都展露着时代的风彩。

精工牌
SEIKO

精工表维修网点：北 京·天 津·西 安·哈尔滨·沈 阳·青 岛·上 海·广 州·福 州

商务画册　　出类拔萃

商务印书馆香港分馆·北京故宫博物院
动员大量人力物力财力，历时五载，
出版划时代的大型画册
《紫禁城宫殿》、《国宝》和《清代宫廷生活》，
综合介绍故宫博物院的建筑、藏品
和宫廷史迹文物三大内容。

获香港市政局
主办1982年度
最佳印制中文艺术书籍奖
英文版获香港市政局
主办1984年度
全年最佳印制书籍奖及
最佳印制英文美术书籍奖

获香港市政局
主办1983年度
最佳印制中文美术书籍奖

《紫禁城宫殿》
于倬云主编
介绍紫禁城宫殿宏伟壮丽的
建筑群
图片467幅·文字8万·332页
8开·精装·定价港币480元
1982年出版

《国宝》
朱家溍主编
展示故宫九十一万件藏品中
精选出来的百件珍品
图片274幅·文字10万·264页
8开·精装·定价港币480元
1983年出版

《清代宫廷生活》
万依　王树卿　陆燕贞主编
彻底揭露森严神秘的清代帝
王生活
图片500幅·文字11万·328页
8开·精装·定价港币480元
1985年出版

 商务印书馆香港分馆

总办事处 ● 香港鰂鱼涌芬尼街2号D侨英大厦五楼
电话 ● 5-651371-6　电报 ● COMPRESS(或5364)　电传 ● 86564 CMPRS HX

有朋远方来，喜乘三菱牌

国际影坛上的香港女明星张曼玉。三菱汽车常同她一起，在许多银幕中登场，而且三菱车已成为她在日常生活中所不可缺少的伙伴。三个钻石的商标占据着她整个生活中的一个重要部分。

在银幕中，她不断塑造各种人物形象，而三菱汽车则同人们的生活息息相关。可见车子是她最可靠的合演者，又是她生活中最得力的同伴。

三菱汽车昼夜奔驰在世界上130个国家的道路上，在为人们创造更美好的生活中，发挥着应有作用。面向中国的三菱车是根据使用要求和用途制造的，帮您创造新生活，载您驰骋四化园。

三个钻石商标的汽车，今日又会使您笑逐颜开………。

三菱 T850 大型卡车　　三菱 PAJERO

三菱汽车

RESEARCH

日立公司正在研究开发中的技术
（从左到右）：电脑层析Ｘ射线摄
影法、激光、机器人、电脑扫描
人眼以及光学圆盘存储器。

七十五年来，日立公司一本"以先进技术为全世界服务"的精神，孜孜不倦地推动研究开发工作。我公司的各研究机构，在广泛的领域内，开发独创性的技术，革新电气与电子产品，供全球各地的家庭、办公室、学校及医院采用。

最近，日立公司又成立第二十一所研究开发中心，叫做先进研究实验室，以便开发为二十一世纪提供服务的长期应用研究项目。

各项成果俯拾即是

我公司的激光技术实现了以光学圆盘文件存储方式高密度地记录业务数据。由于机器人技术不断改进，极复杂的生产工艺也能自动化。日立公司的新型图象与伴音系统，活用数字技术，为您提供超高保真度伴音及高清晰度电视图象。

日立公司每年投下约一亿美元的研究费用。我们拥有一万六千名研究开发人员，为发展先进技术，贡献力量。

同时，向世界各地提供三万五千件专利，与各国人民分享新知识所带给人类的成果。

开创最完美的未来世界

展望未来世界，机器翻译系统将大力而急速地促进各国之间的文化交流。为了适应今后的能源需要，我们正在开发核聚变系统；我们也在研究利用超导磁场以每小时300哩的高速离地浮起疾驶的电车，及医学诊断用三维彩色扫描设备与仿真手术等等技术。

随着技术的进步，各种机器也日益复杂化。日立公司努力研究技术高深复杂而便于操作使用的各项产品，使人与机器更加融会贯通。经由此等研究工作，我们相信必能适应人们的需要，并进一步提高全人类的生活水平。

我们相信研究为进步之母。